How Mar

Written by Cassie Bell

Photographed by Francis Zera

How many boxes do you see?

Three.

How many apples do you see?

Four.

How many jars do you see?

Two.

How many dogs do you see?

One.

How many cans do you see?

Five.

How many children do you see?

Two.

Two sticky ones!